Keeping Them Alive

To Maddie
Thanks for your great
work.

Keeping Them Alive

Poems by Christine Stewart-Nuñez

Christine Stewart Nuñez

WordTech Editions

Norgren ECU Harrington
Contest 2014

Published by WordTech Editions
P.O. Box 541106
Cincinnati, OH 45254-1106

ISBN: 9781936370238
LCCN: 2010942674

Poetry Editor: Kevin Walzer
Business Editor: Lori Jareo

Visit us on the web at www.wordtechweb.com

For Holden—my beautiful boy—
and in memory of my sister,
Theresa (1964-1984)

Acknowledgments

My thanks to Dorianne Laux, Greg Glazner, Hilda Raz, Ted Kooser, Rochelle Harris, Marianne Zarzana, Carrie Shipers, Darla Biel, Patrick Hicks, Diane Frank, Sara Olivier, Jonis Agee and the Nebraska Summer Writers Conference, South Dakota State University's Department of English and College of Arts and Sciences (Griffith Award Grant), SDSU's Research and Scholarship Support Fund, and my family.

I am grateful to the editors of the following publications in which these poems first appeared or were reprinted:

American Life in Poetry (#249. 27 Dec. 2009): "Convergence"

Atlanta Review (16.1, 2009): "Ode at Twenty-One Weeks"

Briar Cliff Review (21, 2009): "Convergence"

Calyx: A Journal of Art and Literature by Women (25.2, 2009): "In Praise of a Pregnant Body"

Chickenpinata: A Journal of Poetry (5, 2010): "Exposure"

The Evansville Review (18, 2008): "Nursing"

Green Hills Literary Lantern (15, 2004): "Continuation"

A Harvest of Words: Contemporary South Dakota Poetry (Center for Western Studies, 2010): "Seven Spills," "Ode at Twenty-One Weeks," "Meditation on the Smallest Bone in the Body," "Convergence"

The Iguana Review (9, 2009): "Inside the Spin"

Paddlefish (3, 2009): "Defense," "What She'd Say"

Passages North (26.1, 2005): "Upon a Request to Describe the Impact of Her Death" (under the title "Your Death")

Paterson Literary Review (33, 2004): "Instead of Crying, I Turn to Flowers" (under the title "Wake")

Prairie Schooner (83.4, 2009): "Contemplating Conception, I Write About the Weather," "Meditation on the Smallest Bone in the Body"

South Dakota Review (41.4, 2003): "Blueberry Pancakes"

Sugar House Review (12, 2010): "An Apology to Stay a Greater Loss, with *Demi*"

The Sycamore Review (17.1, 2005): "The Intended" (under the title "At First")

The Texas Review (25.3/4, 2004): "Confession" (under the title "Postscript for My Sister")

Tipton Poetry Journal (2010): "Buddha Laugh"

Valparaiso Poetry Review (11.2, 2010): "Art Lessons"

Table of Contents

Please call me by my true names,
so I can hear all my cries and my laughter at once,
so I can see that my joy and pain are one.
—Thich Nhat Hanh

Braid of Birth and Death in Blue

cracked shell of a robin's egg

cervix after conception

indigo salt

empty casket's pool of navy satin

parallel lines of a pregnancy test

cerulean, Persian, cobalt

steel gray of infant eyes

chant a pitch below cornflower

range of a sister's chameleon eyes

veins like lapis lazuli

beryl, royal, teal

newborn's knitted cap

wool of the Madonna's mantle

illuminated letter in ultramarine

turquoise star ring, a sister's last gift

denim, Prussian, cyan

Sister's lips when Mother found her

azure glass in the chapel where mothers pray

sapphire of a flame's base

midnight umbilical, looped

The temple bell stops but I still hear
the sound coming out of the flowers.
—Matsuo Basho

Contemplating Conception, I Write About the Weather

In a journal—leather-bound, butterfly
embossed—I plan to record symptoms, dreams

as they turn. I write spring. On day three:
Buds point skyward, tongues licking

wind. Daffodils—green wands—push
through dirt, birds chirp from feeders.

I can't commit to paper my attempt to plant
you, as if "you" are definite, already dividing,

a bundle of tumbling proteins. Day seven:
Gray-bottomed clouds against blue sky.

Sleet stings a garden's snowdrops. I long
for warmth. I coach myself to spill

uncensored. Only this: *A brief sun teases.*
Have you cleaved to me? Day fourteen:

Gold crocus open. My body won't
flower. No nausea, breast tenderness,

only an ache in my core. The usual
blood. What words created, life

absorbs, cell like any other cell.

Confession

Sister, you didn't know I pretended
to snore in my Strawberry Shortcake
sleeping bag as you yelled at Mom

across the room. She hissed, Why
do you do this to me? You couldn't see
yourself stumbling up the sidewalk

in your nurse's uniform, bottle
in hand. You reached for me;
I turned away. Beer lessens stress,

you said. Whenever you made
Mom cry, I bit my lip, wished
the worst. How could I have known

when I woke to your unmade
bed and crossed myself to make
the prayer official? As the hum

of your car's engine pulled Mom
to the garage door, as I wished
for you to die, you already had.

Upon a Request to Describe the Impact of Her Death

A relief against which I measure everything:
a phantom twin, unending thread.
Full turn. Water to which I cling.

Bitter honey. Whistle of an evening
train. Feasts of unleavened bread.
A motif with which I measure everything:

unpronounceable vowel, black ruby ring,
last line of every book I've read.
Full. Turn. With water I cling

to a window made of hummingbird wing.
A well sustaining a watershed.
A belief with which I measure everything:

a scratched scar throbs, an overflowing
cup. Song from which my will is fed.
Full. I turn. To water, I cling

and try to sip. A stay against drowning
in exquisite pain. Failure of heart-over-head.
A grief against which I measure everything.
Full, I turn to water, and cling.

In Praise of a Pregnant Body

Some women count calories, step on the altar
of weight each week, mourn the loss of waist—
jeans too tight to button. I prefer to blossom.
I surrender to coconut salmon in banana leaves,
miso soup with prawns, paella, lasagna, seafood
risotto, mangu and tostones, salads of blueberries,
blood oranges, and papaya, the bloom of belly,
breasts spilling over seams, areolas darkening.

I've abandoned the lunch-break park with its tire swing
and picnic of stale chips for a circus of lion tamers,
dogs with purple tutus, magicians pulling doves
from top hats, trapeze artists somersaulting
through the air. I want the Big Top's pillows
of cotton candy dissolving in my mouth, mounds
of popcorn shiny with butter, globes of caramel
apples, hot dogs drenched in mustard.

Blood thickening and milk springing from nipples
remind me: Be open. Enough of this suburb
with its square meals served in look-alike
houses. Give me Paris with its artists scattered
on sidewalks, painted confetti, dancers
from discothèques stretching onto streets at dawn.
With more body to envelop, I'll browse boutiques
at the Rue du St.-Honoré, lounge sipping café-au-lait
and nibbling a croissant's flakey layers. Order coq-au-vin
or pot-au-feu; decorate the board with baguette,
brie. Will mousse aux fraises complete me?

If I'd been born with different genes—

petite, straight-hipped, willowy-tall—would I enjoy
fat bowls of kalamata olives, sliced avocado,
desserts of mangoes in cream, pumpkin pie?

I surrender to possibility, to joy, to feasts
of seven-grain breads, lamb stews, chocolate
soufflés. I thank this baby whose growing bones
demand wheels of provolone, sticks of mozzarella,
cubes of sharp cheddar, cups of vanilla yogurt
at two a.m., whose kicks remind me to taste
roast beef, venison steak, the cream of deviled eggs.

Spot

Two hundred thirty-four periods
trained me to feel my cyclical

shift, to count down before
I welcomed the warm mark,

sometimes its soft ache
inconvenient, sometimes

a thanksgiving. I never
thought its absence a safe

sign, never added days
of lack for peace of mind

until ten weeks pregnant: a spot—
blush of terror.

What color? asked the hotline
nurse. Like wine? Like Christmas?

Lighter, almost pink? I decided
like bricks. Then relax.

A cramp. Read your body,
a book advised. Every five minutes

I slid down my underwear
to gauge betrayal's shade.

Keeping Them Alive

"Birth, life, and death—each took place
on the hidden side of a leaf."
                              —Toni Morrison

Press dirt firmly, give
a good first drink, dust
leaves with a damp cloth—
Mom's ritual for each cutting
clipped from my sister's
funeral plants. My leaves
smattered with yellow spots
droop. I try a western window.
No change. I inspect for the flies
Mom sprays with poison:
If bad, wrench the roots out,
hose off every speck of dirt
and replant in fresh soil. None.
I blame the cold sill.

One of Mom's three
sits in her dining room.
She never prunes when
hibiscus bloom; instead,
she whispers deep inside
the pink trumpets. After
a day they twist close, drop.
She scoops up the fallen,
stroking with a fingernail.

Once, vacationing sea-side,
Mom arranged my brother

and me near a hibiscus hedge
so petals touched our shoulders.
She snapped a photo.

When I find my cutting
with curled leaves in the dirt,
I drive three hours home
with it in my lap. Mom
looks at the stick in the pot,
places her hand on mine.
It's already gone, she says.
There's nothing I can do.

The Horizon Outlines Grief

A silent sinew of air. Tangles
ripple in sunlight, muscles
bamboo flat. Scent
signals typhoon.

Rain burst. A horizon
of gauze, a bluestem
field in dissipating fog.

Listen to a sky of cranes.
Thousands ribbon
down, dissolve
into a membrane
on the river's sand bars.

Ice on this wintered
lake's thinning skin.
Skaters razor patterns
of sound as they circle.

Halley's Comet stencils
midnight every seventy-five
years chalking constellations
with dust. We recognize
it as light.

Measure the density
of ghosts not by the Earth's
curve; memory presses
a cheek, the weight
of a name on our tongues.

This Way of Knowing

1.

Emptied at eleven
years old. Youth opened

its arms and caged me.
Expecting tree rings

I snapped a pencil.
It tickled my ankle,

the fringe of death's
skirt. Sloughed off

in the shower, cells
of old skin. All

these, how a child
apprehends an end.

Knowledge steeps:
water becomes tea,

once acrid leaves
sweet with honey.

2.

Before the fruit knew
its need to loosen,

drop, I could predict
the cold hand's twist,

pluck. This unripe pear's
skin doesn't appear

to blush. I bite. Crunch.
Too soon. Tart, a chunk

falls from my lips.
Under a fingertip's

pressure, ripe flesh
should yield. Brash—

too early do I taste
the white core's grains.

3.

My pudgy hand takes
the spoon of horseradish,

expects whipped cream.
What will sweeten

this baker's cocoa
so bitter in my mouth?

The body reacts
when we're distracted:

I pick at my Band-Aid's
corner. Sister explains

the stars; goose bumps
rise on my arm. She points

to heaven, rips off
my bandage and laughs.

4.

Late July, 108 degrees.
Sandals soak concrete's

heat. Sandwiched between
the wood door and screen

I stand, palms flush, cheek
against green paint. Is she

coming to unlock it? I feel
the other side, cool a/c.

I recall little before Sister's
death, everything after.

The Intended

I'll write about how Mayans transformed
beans of the cocoa plant into powder, when
autumn leaves looked like stilled hands
on hearse windows, the ways bad things
can repeat in families. Spinning events
in my hand must create meaning. I'll be
discursive about day lilies curving
over the blue fence, the smell of cut
cantaloupe, seventy-degree days of sunshine
in November, the suicide of a sweet poet.
Perhaps the scraw and screal of two birds
as they dive to grass will lead me to conclude
it's smart to risk loving. I'll psychoanalyze
the Morse code of a cardinal, the removal
of blueberry stains from white cotton. I'll delete
dreams where my water breaks on my sister's
grave. I'll explain four swallow eggs—
cracked—in a nest outside the window. Did I
succumb to each stage of grief in good time?
Let's praise the potted geranium as a child's ball
blooming in cement, the life cycle of roses,
how some make tea from their hips.

Before the Baby Arrives

> "It is the responsibility of every expectant parent
> to clean out ... the psyche by... resolving inner
> conflicts."
>
> —*Mind Over Labor*

Sister's death: a pain lodged
in my brain, sealed in cells
of lung, in shallow, sporadic
breaths. Skin over breastbone
bruised years ago, still tender.
I gather broom, dustpan, sweep
shards glittering behind my eyes.
This rain of fractured evidence
is grief's broken pane. Instincts
urge flight, fight. Muscles contract.
Her laughter rings out from memory;
glass melts into sand. I exhale.
Fists flower at my sides.

Inside the Spin

Usually when Sister
drove me to band practice

too early, I'd wait, pinned
against the brick wall

by wind. That morning,
snow-covered ice.

Let's do donuts! she
said, blotting red lips.

White knuckled, my fist
clenched the clarinet case.

Eyes opened wide. Picking
up speed the VW hummed;

she slammed the gearshift
into second, braked.

Leather gloves cranked
the wheel. Buildings

blurring around us——still
in the center——we spun.

The Death Card

Meaning: Necessary and profound change.
Everything has its season.

Turned from the spread before me:

a horizon where blue sky meets

red, a brightness below as if sun

burst beneath. On the ground, green

shoots grow from calcified cups

of bone; two sprout hand-shaped

flowers. I am this smiling skeleton,

my skull one she dances upon.

Defense

I was five. I placed twigs
at intervals across sidewalk
cracks; fissures detoured
ants to premature deaths.
I believed bridges saved them.

Skipping through sprinklers, friends
shrieked as icy water nipped
bellies. Teens filled water balloons
playing tag across three lawns.
Bobby hurled one at my sister,

a rock disguised in rubber, water.
Crumpled, she held her leg as a welt
purpled her thigh. Bobby laughed,
clutching his stomach. Then, the iron
rake. Air rocketed out when

I hit him. Did she run to him
or me? Alone, pig-tailed girl
with stubbed toes, I knocked
on his door to apologize,
Mother watching from the street.

An Apology to Stay a Greater Loss, with
Demi

In a café, cappuccino and croissant
at hand, I write *I'm sorry.*
At the next table, a small loaf
in the society of bread—a demi—
distracts. It's enough for dinner
and the next day's sandwiches.
I'll accept more than my share.
I write *Blame* in the saucer
of olive oil. In French peace
is paix. Only next to long loaves
of sourdough does the demi seem
unfinished. The croissant evokes
the crescent of demi-lune where
sun reveals the whole after seven
days; the complete yet not full
demi-tasse; the bra's cut for breasts
whose slopes place nipples just
beneath a lacy rim. Moons, crusts,
cups—my fears of loss, of the miracle
of multiplying loaves, of letters
of regret. Half or whole, in French
bread is pain.

Elephant Stairs

—For Ruby (1973-1998) Elephant, Painter

Climb stairs wide-legged,
two at a time; he'll drop
in your pelvis, the midwife

says. Ruby's fetus, full-term,
punctured her uterine wall.
In gray pants and shirt, I move

like the Asian elephant:
4.5 tons, pregnant in the heat
of Phoenix, poised under trees,

paintbrush lifted. Twelve flights,
twelve days, I lumber under
sixty extra pounds, ten of it baby.

Did Ruby paint as infection
spread? Turquoise arcs, azure
lines, a pool of crimson

in the canvas center as her child
died in her womb? The yellow
line slides to green as the nurse

wheels me to surgery. For Ruby,
c-section was the end. I twist
her blues into breath.

Instead of Crying, I Turn to Flowers

Dry-eyed at Sister's vigil, I scribble
on a receipt from Mom's purse:
Once there was a rose. I slip
notes between satin and suede
in her coffin for safe keeping,
for travel. A classmate hands
me a construction-paper card:
I bleed for you written
under a dripping red heart.

Why is her skin wrinkled?
The car's exhaust was poison
Mom says, her eyes the only
pure parts to donate. I wonder
what they put under her eyelids
to make it look as if they could
flutter open at any minute.
I wrote: *From the dead rose,*
seeds took root, grew.
Mom says her gravestone
will read *Her blue eyes lit*
all our lives. Aren't mine just
as pretty? I wonder if hers
will recognize me.

Blueberry Pancakes

You probably don't remember. The week after
her death, you took me to Ember's. I ordered
pancakes with fruit, my first taste of juice
exploding as I chewed, my first time alone
with a teacher who threw erasers at mouthy
sixth graders. You ordered coffee, black.
Was I supposed to chat with my math teacher,
my sister's favorite bartender? Mistakes. Mine
happened to be adding. You didn't know
how drunk she was that night. Under your gaze,
I placed a napkin across my school uniform
skirt, crossing and uncrossing my ankles.
Did you calculate comfort? The weight
of "I'm so sorry?" I didn't hear anything.
After a sip of milk, I knocked over the salt;
my sleeve got stuck in syrup. Who did
you see looking across the table? People say
we had the same gestures. I wore her—
I mean my—t-shirt advertising your bar
to gym class, promised to visit the day
I turned legal.

Inside the Snow Globe

Bourbon perfumes Father's
pillow. Nose against glass,

my hands pull cold through
the pane. Brother sleeps;

squirt guns, hammers, plastic
soldiers border his bed. Behind

blue and red striped drapes,
breath crystallizes on glass.

In January's blizzard, beacons
from neighbors' windows

flicker. Tip toe. In a recliner,
Mom and I curve, mugs

of cocoa cooling in our hands.
In her robe's collar I nuzzle

my face. The dog slides on ice.
One bad step, the house spins.

In the backyard light's glow,
tornadoes of snowflakes.

Ode at Twenty-One Weeks

Praise the sonogram's glow, the spine's colonnade
of bone from sacrum to skull—tiny cupola—
here soft, round. Praise columns of femur, tibia,
humerus, fingers and toes imagined; praise a hint
of ribs at the nave, black mass inside called "heart."

Praise this technological grisaille, the landscape
in process it renders, sketch called body.
Praise the expanse of skin suggested by shadow,
horizon of earth, sky. Praise the sealed sea
protecting the face: profile's slope, chin's curve, bud
of nose. Praise caves named "liver," "spleen."

Yes, praise this musical hazelnut, mini bass drum
at *prestissimo*, new symphony's first refrain.
Praise the spiraled blue cord, pulsing placenta
echoing the heart's beat. Praise this organ fixed
fast to the acoustical eaves of uterine wall.
Praise the whispered swish, swish.

Praise again, as if an epilogue or epic's choral
refrain, the spine. Praise its white stitches,
binding arc—cervical to pelvic—narrative
start to finish. Praise its interlocking words, chapters
of nerve. Praise it, praise it, this burgeoning book.

Babelfish Translates the Gestation Dream

Afraid to dream, I asked
them to cease and stopped
recalling all except one where
the baby tried to be born
through my belly, pushing
through my skin; alive, crying,
clay-like, the color of cornflowers
and the midnight from which his body
was formed, he struggled to be born.

~

It alarms me to dream so I required
they stop, all but where he drinks,
tries to carry my belly, press over
my skin. He drinks living sailors—
blue like loam. Cornflowers cry
the midnight from which his body
was formed; he stretches to press
through completely, crossing,
(by fighting), in order to be carried.

~

To dream, to stop dreaming.
I remember all but where
the child pushes through my skin,
a dark blue alive child who
demands, who has held increase.
Blue like clay of cornflower,
the midnight from which its body

is made. Hands formed, entirely
born and fighting.

~

Dreaming alarmed me. I asked
that they cease. I recall
all except where it drinks, the baby,
where it tried to push through
womb skin. I drink blue, alive Marín
and cry out, blue as the cornflower
clay, midnight from which his body
was formed. It gives to push through
the passage, fighting to be led.

~

Fear, it dreamed. I asked it to stop
itself. I have myself exactly. I continue
except where the child pressures my belly,
works with shovel of an alive shady blue
child. He is caused. Like midnight cornflower,
he cries out. He whose relative this blue
organism became. Relative the hands
that detect, that completely formed
the child, to be caused, to be combat.

Exposure

A decade later, I develop film
I found in my dead sister's room.
The colors were wrong: browns, greens,
images bleeding. Flashes of light
replace heads. In *Our Town* Emily says,
My life happened a thousand years ago.
The newly dead become eternal,

but the living aren't purged of their loss
quickly. At the corner café, Julia's
eyes tighten when she sees silk tied
around a woman's neck; Henry cries
when he smells Estée Lauder and cigarettes.
A man hunches over two beers every
Friday at Stormy's Bar, one mug
for his twin, missing in Vietnam.

I spread her photos out, label them:
laughing, not laughing, can't tell.
The living dream the long dead
newly so: a suicide cold against
the wheel; stroke victim collapsed
in the shower. Worse, we dream them
alive, chatting over coffee, waving a car
off. Then we wake, expectant, as my sister
in this photo, arms draped over friends'
shoulders, smile anticipating the flash.

Seven Spills

1.

Every mountain I touch I taint
with desert dust, still I climb
for hours, and at the top restrain
the urge to step off. I skim
loose boulders with my boot. Imagine
this beauty, silhouette of a body
poised—arms arc above—to spin,
spill down rock, tree over tree...
Sister, for years after your death
I sought the grace to quit this life,
searched for blazes on my path
of forgetting. Today cliff-side
views whisper a new language,
my shaking feet contained at the edge.

2.

My shaking feet contained at the edge
of Sister's room. I'm nine. Four
elixirs line her window's ledge:
dandelion, cherry, seashore
blue and jade—colors sunlight
casts across the charmed room.
The glamour mirror glows, the sleight-
of-hand supplies—compacts, perfume—
sparkle. Mesmerized, I want
even the hidden peppermint potion
to fuel friends' giggles and enchant
boys. Years later I pop open
the bottles, flush the magic; putrid,
it is only dyed liquid.

3.

It is only dyed liquid
in my childish eye: whiskey,
scotch—father's treats he slides
out of cupboards after three
p.m., amber drops that slosh
as he pours, drip down the shot-glass
like sweat zigzagging across
his rough cheek, shiny as meat grease
on his chin, the shape of the tear
that splashes on his robe with the whisper
"They can't find her pulse" on the clear
November morning Sister
dies. Mom can clean up a spill,
I say, yet we'll feel it still.

4.

I say, Yes, we feel it still.
Smoldering at age six, fed up
with revolving around Sister's will
(find coat, fetch coffee cup),
I plead: Please share your can
of 7 Up. I taste the pop
she poured for me—water. Rather than
laugh with her, I soak her top.
Drops drip from her hair. Such
a supernova. She'd ignite
every room with her hand's touch.
In shadows I feel it still, her light—
luminosity left behind
in the cold core, one binary blind.

5.

In the cold core, one binary blind;
so young, I knew her as sister only.
I asked: What sort of woman, what kind
of friend was she? With everyone she
met, she lined up her cards, turned
them over; she looked people in the eye.
With kings collected first, she learned
to play them last, throwing the die
to win: Raise your bets, guard
your hand. This strength I sought
to walk away from her house of cards
collapsed. Numbers tumbling, she taught
Spite & Malice when she played
with old folks as a white-smocked aide.

6.

At the old folks' home: white-smocked aides,
crested nurses. A silver-haired woman
curls her fingers around a tray's
sterling rim. Into her open
mouth I spoon food. She supervises
this supper, my sister, darting between
clients, her reflection in the sides
of wheelchairs. Ladle in, clean
up, turn out—she's smiling, always.
A bowl drops. Voices hush.
Accidents happen, Sister says.
Peas trickle out of the woman's lips,
dribble down the white cardigan;
now green her pale, translucent skin.

7.

Now green her pale, translucent skin
I write, the tip of the silver ball-point
turning blue. Ink seeps into twin
cells, cities. I blot the print
and the pen explodes, a glacial lake
on this vanity map. With tissue I press—
a pool ripples out in the wake
of words. I've made another mess.
Streaked with ink, my hands. A line
of blue mirrors a snaking vein,
a river across this continent's spine.
Inches of flatland are smudged with stain.
For deserts I'm a veritable saint;
every mountain I touch, I taint.

Trimesters

"Light burst ... like a flower
on the farther side of death."
                    —Hildegard of Bingen

Rain fills
this red cup
of spring,
a tulip
like any other.

~

The solstice, a day
where an egg stands
on end from sunrise
to sunset, the moon
balancing yolk, sac.
I imagine he stops
swimming in sleep,
opens his arms.

~

Leaves turn, first
on branches then
through the air
becoming sound.

Underfoot, they rust.

Son, you fatten, skin
supple over spine.
In months, you
break loose, move
into winter sun,
my hands, this
other light.

Continuation

At Lion's Park, I sit
on a gridiron bench and listen
to swings creak, watch them
sway under a cloudless sky.
Almost winter, geese fly—
a black V against the sun
passing white overhead.
November should be damp,
thunder far off. Air should
smell of flowers' decay.
Instead, her weather: leaves
lemon yellow scraps tipped
orange, brown maples end-
curled, half clinging, some
wind-swept over patched grass.
Near the pool where we played
as kids, the solitary fire bush,
its leaves glowing flames.

Breakfast for Supper

At IHOP, after the skinny brunette
with a band-aid covering her hickey
comes to whisk away burnt toast,
Mom mentions Theresa, face
brightening. She had a dream
about her—80s flip hair, smooth
complexion. I've been living
in Tulsa for eighteen years,
Theresa said. I understand.
Even as I watched men lower
her casket, I fantasized the witness
protection program had resettled her.

How funny we look, mother
and daughter laughing over
scrambled eggs, tears dripping
onto bacon, hands hugging
coffee mugs. For a moment Mom felt
Theresa *there*. Such faith. Freshen
your cup? the waitress asks me, poised
to pour. Cloudy in the cold coffee,
my reflection. I offer the mug.

A Study of Her Hands

Her hands tap dance on teacups'
lips, pluck corn silk, snap beans.

The sound in her hands:
      crinkling tissue of the blouse pattern,
      slice and snip as she clips cloth,
      the hum of the machine's hesitation
      as she adjusts linen under its silver foot.

Her hands pin gingham at three-inch
intervals, upholster davenports.

The art from her hands:
      flour, sugar sifted; eggs, oil whisked;
      icing hand-dyed mauve, goldenrod, aquamarine,
      hundreds of frosting stars squeezed
      for Holly Hobby's calico dress.

Her hands still the toddler's
tornado, scrub scum from bathtubs.

She stays his drinking with the labor of her hands:
      slices braised roast beef,
      bakes dinner rolls before factory work,
      grills pork chops the size of the New Testament,
      unzips peas from buttered pods.

Her hands pack one-thousand
boxes, pick ticks from puppies.

The rebellion of her hands:

nerves tingle, stabbing from ring finger
to thumb. Numbness. Olive jar dropped.
Spheres roll across linoleum,
pimentos sticking out like tongues.

Her hands soap curses from
mouths, diaper a disabled friend.

She tugs the forty-year-old diamond ring from her finger,
    recites her grandmother's recipe, then cuts
    shortening with flour, forks the mixture
    until blended, rolls out the disk
    of dough with a wooden pin.

Her hands finger flaws
in organza, dress a dead daughter.

In the photo taken in Italy, she watches churchgoers
    pebble Siena's piazza, a mosaic for God.
    One palm cups her chin, the other spoons
    gelato. After, she pauses for prayer. Her hands
    will be unburdened someday, open to receive.

After Being Asked to Describe Motherhood

Joy that strengthens the fragile bough.
Question embodied, white vine.
Full turn. The body to which I bow.

Sacks of Spanish saffron. Chanted vow
of midnight saints. Water-turned-wine.
Sun that strengthens the fragile bough.

The Sacred Guffaw. Sunrise on the brow
of Loess Hills. Snail's spiral design.
Full turn. The body to which I bow.

Waterfall of autumn leaves. The Tao.
Womb's butterfly, heart on the line.
Hope that strengthens the fragile bough.

Blizzard of flame. Century's here-and-now
in this pearl of flesh, divine.
Full turn. The body to which I bow.

Awe. Winged windows open now
for this First Note, First Flight, First Sign.
Rain that strengthens the fragile bough.
Full turn. This boy to whom I bow.

Nursing

He navigates day,
night by smell,

milk the source
of first dreams.

Moon-blessed sleep.
Before I wake, cries

tug blue-veined
breasts. Plath's words

cow-heavy. Foreign,
this urgent, erotic

hunger. Nipples tingle.
Heat. Full-body

rush. An unexpected
intimacy. He latches.

Listen: swish, swish
a sea-born suction.

We float. Salt lines
leave honey-lace

on cheek, on breast.
His breath between

cream and bread.
Only space shared

now, this lock
of baby to body.

Meditation on the Smallest Bone in the Body

Secure in the middle ear, the *stapes*:
two to three millimeters long
in the common human, size
of a peppercorn or ladybug's
wing, length of a prominent
freckle on my left hand but looped.

Translation: stirrup. Smells of saddle leather
and the hay-sweet heat of horses' coats fill
the air. A gurney with steel legs appears,
the kind the midwife outlawed for my son's
birth, he who shifts in sleep wrapped against
my chest. When she showed us photos

of pushing positions, he heard blood
whooshing, intestines gurgling,
(cochlea, canals new, stirrups
quavering) my voice muffled
by amniotic fluids, waters like those
from which ears—once gills—evolved.

Shorter than a rice grain, the human
stirrup; how miniscule then, the ossicles
of the *Hadrocodium wui*. Alive 195
million years ago, this mammal
the size of a paper clip was saddled
with a modern animal's middle ear,

big brain. The fossil suggests evolutionary
bonds: stirrup as stimulus, intelligence

conductor. A newborn's heart rate slows
when his mother speaks: my ears cup
his fussing. I hear him when we're apart:
espresso machine, sirens, a meow.

They tether us—the curves of his ears—
his cries rope in the loop of need. Follow
the folds, miniatures of mine; within, stirrup,
anvil, hammer vibrate, shift his pitch and rhythm
so I distinguish pain from hunger, boredom
from fear. This smallest, this strongest bone.

Still Life Snapshots

Before, I studied blushing pears at rest
in an oval bowl, polished grapes
kissing mahogany. Now sun spills
between window blinds brightening
cat hair on the couch where my husband
reads about childbirth, his knees a table.
Pen in hand, muscles along his spine
pulse as if ideas make noise.
Like an augur, his bare foot curls.

~

My husband whispers
to one he knows, lips
to belly, skin a conduit,
goose bumps conducting
music through fine hairs:
I can't wait to see you.
A kick—vibration
on the drum of body,
kiss to belly to cheek.

~

Urgent cries rouse us, trinity
alone. My husband unwinds
the infant from layers of cotton.

Fasteners rip, the Whoa! as he steps
back—gut-punched by pungent
baby shit. Soaked diaper aside,
cloth in hand, he stares at meconium
between kicking legs. Baby's
face reddens, working into a wail.

Dead Sisters

Bedrooms are empty
where they once painted
eyelids, dabbed Cinnabar behind ears,
flipped back layers with curling wands,
but it doesn't mean they're lost.
Sisters never leave forever, memory
just changes the record,
Bee Gees swapped for early AC/DC.
Remember *Gray's Anatomy*, boot cut Levi's,
and leather coats even if dreams replace
plaid with white cotton, if morning wipes
lipstick off the cigarette.

In Tuscany I kept seeing
my twenty-year-old sister
in her early forties. She sipped Chianti,
nibbled on a plate of gnocchi,
introduced herself
as Cristina or Terri. Eyes
brightening, she toured Siena
and Rome with me.

I was a child when she died;
I've forgotten her walk, voice.
In my dreams she's seven
feet tall, freckles misplaced.
Through castles she tromps,
soaping carriage windows, slaying
dragons. Princes beg for her hand.

What She'd Say

Little sister, you think too much, nose in books, finger
pushing up glasses. You analyze the impact
buying cotton made in India has on the war
in Iraq. Remember spaghetti fights, our schnauzer's
birthday cake baked in a plastic play oven,
hollering at boys in Camaros? I'm proud
of your degrees, but I like you best when
you've just finished making love, when you fall
out of your chair laughing, when you sip
Ketel One on the rocks with four limes
between stints on the dance floor. I applauded
when you yelled at the jackass who didn't allow
his preschooler to pee before ordering at Wendy's.
Even when alive, I worried where thoughts
would take you. I watch when you pace, cry
yourself to sleep. When nightmares move across
your body, I put silence in your open mouth.

Scar

Thirty years from now, my son might
ask to see the scar where the surgeon
wiggled him out. Hand against his forehead,
my pelvic bone trapped him. One hundred
years ago, certain death, the doctor said.
Believe me: I didn't want a nurse to count
out scalpels, see the searing white of gloved
hands, my body numb from breast to toe.

At forty weeks with no show, midnight
contractions vanishing at sunrise, the technician
coated my belly with gel. Length, fluid
volume measured. She strummed the desk
with long red nails. *10 lbs +*
she scribbled, scissoring off a photo,
a face we'd defined in dreams obscured
by a wave, permanent salute. Strong
she declared the tempo of his heartbeat's
thump, swoosh. As a sigh slipped
from her lips, I smelled a tinge of steel.

The baby's shoulders could wedge,
the midwife said; If your intuition says
caesarian, let's schedule it. I heard
nothing. His father wiped sweat
on his jeans. Two weeks later I listened
through thirty hours of labor. My cervix
locked at five, the mouth of an egg cup,
Baby's head not pressing down enough.
Then I gave in to understanding. When
he cries, my purple line tingles.

Buddha Laugh

A smirk untying the bow
of my son's lips, usual.
Skeptical at eight
weeks. A "hokey pokey"
routine puffs his cheeks,
earns a slim grin.

A friend's baby coos
at blank walls, lifts
eyebrows at a plain
curtain. Ancestors
entertain him, she says.

A Navajo professor
explains: Children live
in the world of the holy
people until their first
laughs—a move toward
the realm of earth.

I recall these stories when
we play "catch," my hands
over my son's. A cascade
of giggles begins in his belly
each time the ball appears.
He nods to new rhythm, tips
of pea-sized toes vibrating.

Art Lessons

At school I never learned the circle, line.
We traced hands to make turkeys and drew
half a heart on a fold, each Valentine
creased. "Contrast" meant yellow with blue.
At home I followed Mom's project design:
cut with care around the pattern tissue,
stitch felt teeth onto a shark-puppet's face,
trim French-knotted pillows with lace.

~

A gift from Mom my first Halloween
at college: a five by five inch cotton sachet
stuffed with cloves, cinnamon. A velveteen
ribbon connected corners. On display:
pumpkins cross-stitched in orange with green
stems still on the vine. *I wanted to pray
for you*, she wrote on a Post-it note affixed,
so I did with each of the 3,300 stitches.

~

November. Six months shy of twenty-one
I sewed words in variegated thread—
shades of blue—as clouds spun
sheets of rain outside. My friend
was dead. I caressed ribbons we'd won,
"Snow Birds" for clarinets stuck in my head.
Her mom requested a square, not song,
for a memory quilt. I stitched until dawn.

~

Non-representational an artist might say,
the memory of the spool. But I see
body, luminous in lines of gray,
black. One thread, one strand free
of shadow, crossed, spiraled, turned away:
scar with bridge of flesh, kidney,
fingernail, lips, triangle above thighs,
thumbprint. The irises of her eyes.

Tidy Habits

A 19th century lantern lifted to light
Iowa coal mines, yellowed-sail model
clipper ship, tequila bottle with worm
suspended. Mom insisted on chores
before play, so every Saturday morning
for a decade I dusted them off.

Now my toddler yells "bean up," tosses
dinosaurs in a box, stacks books,
blocks; his joy of order. Mine, habit:
the impulse to mow overgrown lawns,
scrub down plastic play sets. My hands
have never used saw, level, yet I reach

to repair a sagging porch, replace
sunken stairs. Twice I found empty cans
at my sister's grave, stale Budweiser
on their rims. Once a bundle of daisies
tied with yarn, a clutch of red carnations.
Vase up in spring, down in winter.

Someday I'll tell my son: leave
dishes in the sink for morning, put
a book or two in every room. After
I die, scatter my dust. Let it settle
in lilacs with the rush of spring.
Cut a sprig off; take me with you.

Convergence

Through the bedroom window
a February sunrise, fog suspended
between pines. Intricate crystals—
hoarfrost lace on a cherry tree.
My son calls out, awake. We sway,
blanket-wrapped, his head nuzzling
my neck. Hoarfrost, tree—I point,
shaping each word. Favorable
conditions: a toddler's brain, hard
data-mining, a system's approach.
Hoar, he hears. His hand reaches
to the wallpaper lion. Phenomena
converge: warmth, humidity,
temperature's sudden plunge;
a child's brain, objects, sound.
Eyes widening, he opens his mouth
and roars.

Notes

The book's epigraph is taken from the poem "Please Call Me By My True Names" (*Please Call Me By My True Names: The Collected Poems of Thich Nhat Hanh*, 1999).

"Confession"
After Robin Becker's "Late Words for My Sister" (*The Horse Fair*, 2000).

"In Praise of a Pregnant Body"
After Diane Wakoski's "Ode to a Lebanese Crock of Olives" (*Emerald Ice: selected poems 1962-1987*, 2005).

"Keeping Them Alive"
The epigraph commonly attributed to Toni Morrison, but the source isn't known.

"The Intended"
After Hilda Raz's "Avoidance" (*Trans*, 2001).

"Before the Baby Arrives"
The epigraph is a quote taken from *Mind Over Labor* by Carl Jones (1988).

"Elephant Stairs"
Ruby was an Asian elephant who lived at the Phoenix Zoo. Her paintings sold for up to $5,000 in the 1980s. She died after an attempt to breed her in captivity.

"Exposure"
The words attributed to Emily paraphrase her dialog in Act Three of Thorton Wilder's *Our Town* (1938).

"Trimesters"
The epigraph is taken from Hildegard of Bingen's
"Alleluia-verse for the Virgin" found in *Symphonia: a
critical edition of the Symphonia armonie celestium* translated
by Barbara Newman (1988).

"A Study of Her Hands"
A companion creative nonfiction piece to this poem was
published as "The Work of Hands" (*South Dakota Review*,
Fall 2009).

"Nursing"
The phrase "cow heavy" is taken from Sylvia Plath's
"Morning Song" (*Ariel*, 1966).

"Meditation on the Smallest Bone in the Body"
With thanks to the article "Tiny creature may be ancestor
of all mammals" posted on May 24, 2001 by CNN.com for
many of the scientific facts on which this poem is based.

"Dead Sisters"
With thanks to Carol Muske-Duke's poem "Ionic"
(*Sparrow*, 2003).

CPSIA information can be obtained at www.ICGtesting.com
Printed in the USA
LVOW101343150412

277635LV00001B/46/P